BIFERNO · TRIGNO · SANGRO · MORO · RAPIDO

'ONE MORE RIVER'

THE STORY OF
THE EIGHTH INDIAN DIVISION

ARNO · SENIO · SANTERNO · PO · ADIGE

The Naval & Military Press Ltd

Published by

The Naval & Military Press Ltd
Unit 5 Riverside, Brambleside
Bellbrook Industrial Estate
Uckfield, East Sussex
TN22 1QQ England

Tel: +44 (0)1825 749494

www.naval-military-press.com

In reprinting in facsimile from the original, any imperfections are inevitably reproduced and the quality may fall short of modern type and cartographic standards.

"*PASHA*". *Major-General* DUDLEY RUSSELL, C.B., C.B.E., D.S.O., M.C., *Commanding* EIGHTH INDIAN DIVISION.

The Eighth Indian Division in Italy

17TH INFANTRY BRIGADE.
1st Royal Fusiliers. 1/12th Frontier Force Regiment. 1/5th Royal Gurkha Rifles. (F.F.)

19TH INFANTRY BRIGADE.
1/5th Essex Regiment. (Replaced by 1st Argyll and Sutherland Highlanders.) 3/8th Punjab Regiment. 6/13th Royal Frontier Force Rifles.

21ST INFANTRY BRIGADE.
5th Royal West Kent Regiment. 1/5th Mahratta Light Infantry. 3/15th Punjab Regiment.

ADDITIONAL UNITS.
5th Royal Mahratta Machine Gun Battalion. 1st Jaipur Infantry.

DIVISIONAL RECONNAISSANCE REGIMENT.
6th Duke of Connaught's Own Lancers.

ARTILLERY.
3rd Field Regiment, R.A. 52nd Field Regiment, R.A. 53rd Field Regiment, R.A. 26th Light A.A. Regiment, R.A. 5th Mahratta Anti-Tank Regiment, Indian Artillery.

ENGINEERS.
7th Field Company, I.E. 66th Field Company, I.E. 69th Field Company, I.E. 47th Field Park Company, I.E. (all Bengal Sappers and Miners).

MEDICAL SERVICES.
29th Field Ambulance. 31st Field Ambulance. 33rd Field Ambulance. 20th Indian Field Hygiene Section.

ELECTRICAL AND MECHANICAL ENGINEERS.
120th, 121st and 122nd Indian Mobile Workshops. Divisional Recovery Company. Divisional Gun Repair Section.

ROYAL INDIAN ARMY SERVICE CORPS.
8th D.T.T. Company. 17th I.B.T. Company. 19th I.B.T. Company. 21st I.B.T. Company.

MISCELLANEOUS SECTIONS.
Divisional Ordnance Field Park. Divisional Provost Company. Divisional Postal Section. Divisional Field Cashier.

'ONE MORE RIVER'

THERE have always been rivers ahead of the Eighth Indian Division.

The Division came into this war along the most ancient rivers of all, the Tigris and the Euphrates. In 1941, the ruler of Iraq, with the promise of German support, planned a treacherous attack upon Great Britain, who had freed his country twenty-three years before. The 17th Brigade therefore left Delhi in May, to guard British-owned oilfields in the Mosul villayet. In July and August of the same year, 18th and 19th Brigades followed across the Arabian Sea, to protect the great oil refineries on the Persian Gulf. Here the 18th Brigade fought a three days action against the Iranians, which ended in comic opera fashion when the brass band of the enemy offered to play the victors into occupation of the disputed town.

In October, the three Brigades of the Division, under Major-General C. O. Harvey, C.B., C.B.E., C.V.O., M.C., met at Kirkuk, in northern Iraq, where gas jets from the earth burn unceasingly. A month later, it moved to the northern limits of the oilfields. The Germans were marching with giant strides towards the Caucasus. Should they burst across these mountains, they must be met and held before they reached the waste lands which yielded the precious petroleum. Here the 6th D.C.O. Lancers joined the Division, which set about the digging of fortifications.

In the spring of 1942, the British Eighth Army and the Axis forces were preparing for a decisive encounter in the

Libyan desert south of Tobruk. The enemy under General Rommel attacked on May 26th. On June 13th the battle took a disastrous turn, and the Eighth Army, fighting grimly, withdrew for over four hundred miles into the bottleneck of El Alamein. Rommel lashed his divisions in pursuit, intent on seizing the great prize of the Nile. In late June, the 18th Brigade was given most of the Divisional transport to hurry away on a thousand mile trek across the deserts. Without opportunity to reorganize or reconnoitre, it came into the path of the enemy advance on the morning of July 1st, at Dir El Shein, not far from El Alamein station. The German panzers arrived at noon, demanded and were refused surrender. A dust storm allowed the enemy tanks to close. By nightfall the Essex, the Sikhs and the Gurkhas were overrun and destroyed. The 18th Brigade was never reformed.

The Russians stood at Stalingrad and our oilfields were safe. The Eighth Division withdrew to near Baghdad,

THREE BRIGADIERS

Brigadier (now Maj-Gen.) C. H. BOUCHER, C.B.E., D.S.O. and bar.

Brigadier T. S. DOBREE, C.B.E., D.S.O. and bar, M.C. and bar.

Brigadier B. S. MOULD, D.S.O., O.B.E., M.C.

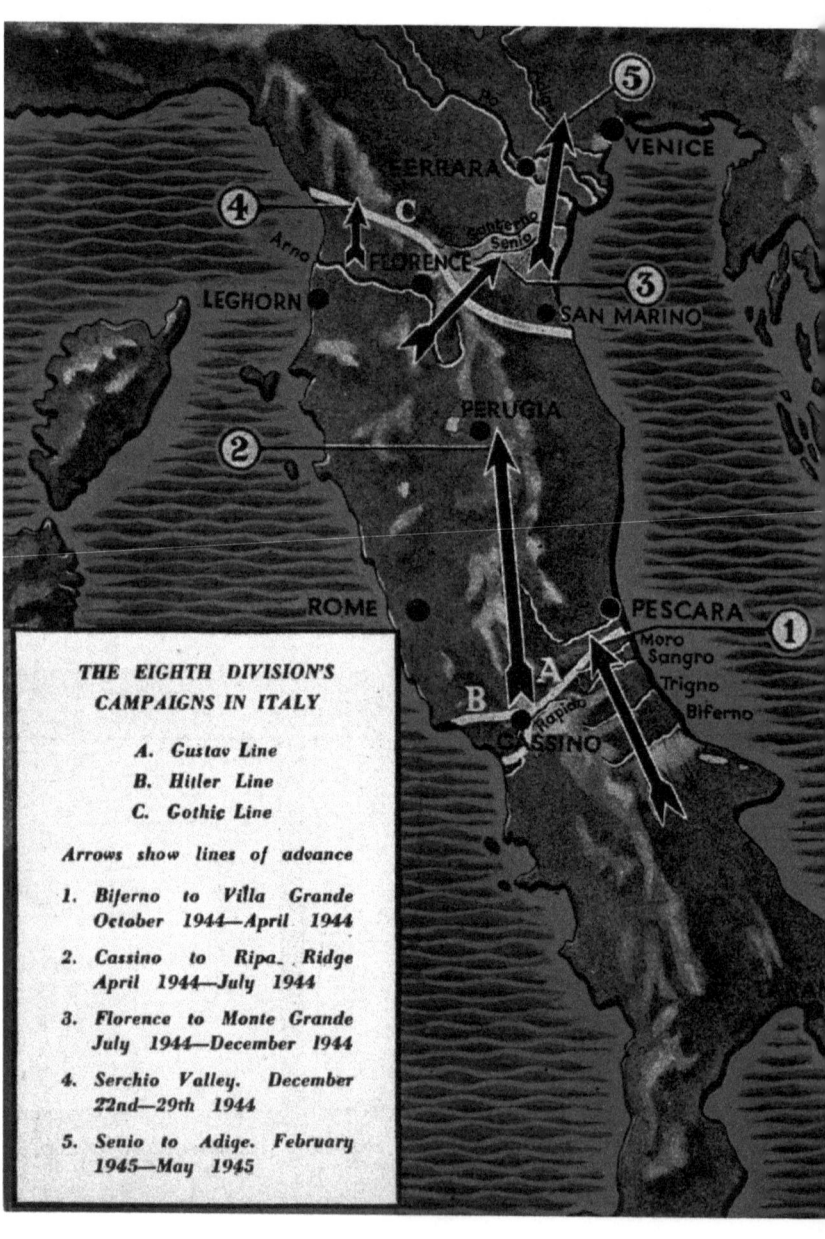

where the 21st Brigade, the 3rd, 52nd and 53rd Field Regiments completed its infantry and gun strength. In January, 1943, Major-General D. Russell, D.S.O., O.B.E., M.C., came out of the Western Desert to take command. He brought a great store of battle knowledge, and he brought luck as well; for within two months the Division was on its way out of the bleak wastes into the green and fruitful land of Syria. In May it reached Damascus and the war grew nearer. For in that month there had been a mass surrender of enemies in Tunisia. To find further Germans to destroy, it would be necessary to cross into Europe.

In June, the Eighth Division was ordered to seize the island of Rhodes, the chief enemy stronghold in the Aegean. Before this plan could fructify, the Eighth Army had swept through Sicily, and had leapt the narrow straits into Italy itself. The Italians capitulated, but their German masters refused to leave, continuing to hold the Kingdom in great force. The Rhodes enterprise therefore was abandoned, and the Eighth Division was warned for service in Europe.

On September 19th, a fleet of six liners stood out from Alexandria, bearing the men of the Eighth Indian Division. Five days later the troopships anchored in Taranto, a harbour in the instep of the foot of Italy.

It so happens, that although Italy everywhere is well-watered and full of streams, in the foot and ankle of the Kingdom the rivers tend to empty towards the south. They thus ran parallel to the line of the Allied advance, and so constituted no great obstacle. But one hundred and twenty-five miles north of Taranto, where the ankle begins to swell into a calf, a mountain chain appears in the centre of the peninsula. These mountains create watersheds, which direct the Italian rivers to the east and west, into the Adriatic and the Tyrrhenian seas. Such rivers were barriers in the path of the Allies, for it is an ancient axiom that water is a surer shield than stone walls, and that a river is a trench in which nature fights for the defenders. When the Germans reached that part of Italy where successive rivers gave them natural defences, they stood at bay, and began to devise fortifications which would make their positions secure.

Our forces were not unprepared. They had brought assault and storm boats, which could be used either to convey troops or as pontoons to support bridges. They brought Bailey Bridge sections, which grew magically into complete spans able to bear great weights. They brought tracked and armoured boats and swimming tanks, and companies of men specially trained to use such equipment. Indeed, bridgement had been developed into a major military science, ingenious and intricate. Yet in mid-October, when the Eighth Division mustered on the line of its first river barrier, it lacked nearly every essential item of bridging equipment. In what has come to be accepted as the British fashion, it was necessary first to improvise, then to wait, then to implore, and finally to receive.

One hundred and fifty miles north of Taranto, the Biferno, a minor stream, covers the approaches to the Trigno, a more substantial river. Here the Bengal Sappers and Miners advanced to tasks which were to become commonplace to them—the clearing of river approaches of mines and booby traps, the bridging of the river, the search of the far bank for any obstacles which might impede the establishment of a bridgehead. On October 21st, the 1st Royal Fusiliers of the 17th Brigade crossed the Biferno and occupied high

DIVISIONAL TRANSPORT passing through a typical Italian Town.

PUNJABI MUSSULMANS move along a stream under smoke cover.

ground. The 1/12th Frontier Force Regiment and the Gurkhas passed through them and pressed on towards the road junction at Palata. A rearguard of paratroopers melted into the darkness when the Mussulmans charged with their age-old war cry " Mara Nara Haidri Ya Ali ". On October 26th, the 19th Brigade leapfrogged through and seized two villages commanding approaches to the Trigno. The opposition stiffened; across the river, on high ground, the village of Tufillo was strongly held. Moreover, the weather worsened; cold winter rains, with driving sleet, transformed the fields into quagmires, the roads into sloughs. On November 2nd, in the dark hours before dawn, the 19th Brigade essayed the crossing. Savage fighting followed. The leading battalions were pinned down, but that afternoon reinforcements closed up. A second night of bitter fighting enabled the 6/13th Royal Frontier Force Rifles, which had led the attack, to break into the enemy's main position. Yet not many of this battalion remained unhurt. The enemy, when their tracer fired the haystacks, became aware of how few continued to attack. The Germans charged and all but closed. Whereupon Subedar Sowar Khan called for defensive fire to fall on his own position, shrewdly realizing that the Germans in the open must suffer more than his own men in their trenches. The enemy broke and ran. Next morning Tufillo was clear, and the Trigno had been forced.

In this first engagement everyone learned that next to courage and skill in battle, what mattered most was the adaptability and resource of the supply services. During the three days of the Trigno fighting, not even a jeep could reach the forward area. The 19th Brigade was maintained entirely by Indian mule transport companies, who faced and

overcame every hazard of the battlefield. After Tufillo was cleared the only routes for wheeled transport were a village street as steep as a staircase, on which vehicles had to be winched up, and lined down; and a mud skidway, on which vehicles slid, ski fashion, down the hillside. A senior officer of another division refused to believe that the Eighth Division could be maintained on such communications.

During this Trigno fighting the 17th Brigade had been loaned to the 78th British Division, which crossed the river on its lower reaches. A series of brisk little fights carried this Brigade well into the twenty miles of broken and precipitous terrain which separates the Trigno from the next river, the Sangro. In this operation the Gurkhas, on the night of November 12th, came stealthily upon the village of Attesa, less than five miles from the Sangro. The village was held by fanatical paratroopers. A wild Donnybrook ensued, but the kukris would not be denied. By dawn every German had run, died, or was in the bag. On its own divisional front the 19th Brigade had continued to clear the path to the Sangro. For three days and nights the 6/13th Royal Frontier Force Rifles battled for the high ground around Archi, only two miles from the river. The 3/8th Punjabis came a mile nearer when they seized Perano, with the aid of New Zealand guns and tanks. These fierce encounters were but prologue to the curtain rising for the main assault.

BREN GUN CREW behind smoke screen before crossing a track during a patrol.

Smoke covers the MAHRATTAS' crossing of the SANGRO river.

The formidable Sangro position might have been designed by a military engineer, so perfectly was it sited for defence. The southern approaches to the river were flat and open. The river itself was 300 yards wide. On the northern bank the ground sloped back to a ridge crowned by five villages of which Mozzagrogna was the key. These villages had been turned into hedgehog positions, with shelters twenty feet deep, with machine-gun posts and covered trenches proof against the heaviest shelling. To storm such fortifications called for great strength. As the forward positions were in full view of the enemy, all preparations for the attack had to be perfected by night. Great dumps of ammunition were established in the forward zone under effective camouflage, for the ten additional field regiments which supplemented the divisional artillery. Tanks, anti-tank guns and machine-gun sections were ordered to cross with the infantry. Powerful air support was laid on.

On November 23rd, in the dense darkness of 0300 hours, the 19th Brigade assaulted Calvario. Fierce and fluctuating fighting followed. The Sangro rose four feet, isolating the troops which had obtained a footing on the northern bank. But within thirty-six hours, a flank for the main attack was secured. The other brigades meanwhile were on their way across the river, in full view of the enemy. Shaken by the fierce bombardment, the Germans chose to await the main assault on the crest of the ridge, in the midst of their maze of defences.

At midnight on November 27th, the Gurkhas and the Royal Fusiliers crept forward. Then followed for two nights and a day a battle in which men fought to the death from alley to alley, from house to house; in which battalion

draftsmen leapt down with kukris to slay a cellarful of Germans; in which an officer from a church steeple fought a single handed duel with an enemy tank; in which panzer grenadiers, veterans of Stalin-
grad, were destroyed in hand to hand combat among the wine casks of the vintage crypts; in which the 50th Royal Tank Regiment had the luck to come upon German armour facing the wrong way at point blank distances.

A memorable episode occurred in Mozzagrogna Square. The situation had grown so critical that orders for withdrawal reached both the Royal Fusiliers and the Gurkhas. The Gurkhas could not withdraw; the Royal Fusiliers would not, until they had extricated their Indian comrades. "Run, Johnny", they shouted, and pinned the German spandau teams in their nests with covering fire. In small groups the Gurkhas dashed across the open, four out of every five making their way to safety.

By the morning of November 30th, the enemy had had enough and the 21st Brigade and 6th D.C.O. Lancers were

able to advance five miles and seize Lanciano, near the main highway to Ortona. The Sangro line was broken. Field Marshal Montgomery sent exultant congratulations to the Eighth Indian Division.

The next river, the Moro, was less than five miles beyond Lanciano. Here Canadians and New Zealanders

MADRASSI SIGNALMEN lay cables in a shattered Italian village.

MAHRATTA MORTAR DETACHMENTS *in action.*

attacked with the Indians demonstrating to deceive the enemy. General Russell ordered part of this deception to be the construction of the "Impossible Bridge", at a right-angled bend in the  ravine of the Moro, a bridge it was necessary to build, and to launch from the enemy's side of the river. The attack on the Moro went in on December 6th. Within seventy-two hours the fighting became so bitter that the Eighth Indian Division was sent to the aid of the men from the Dominions. On November 9th, in the midst of attack and counter-attack, the 3/15th Punjabis crossed "Impossible Bridge" and joined the fray. With the Punjabis went teams of the 5th Mahratta Machine Gun Battalion, under Lieut.-Colonel D. S. Brar, one of the first Indian officers to command a combatant unit in the field. These ultra-keen machine gunners, arriving before their guns, charged with the bayonet beside the Punjabis.

Three days later, 17th and 21st Brigades attacked with Caldari and the line of the Ortona-Orsogna highway as objectives. Day by day more battalions were committed to a wild battle in which infantry, guns and tanks fought doggedly for every yard. The Canadians were heavily engaged on the right flank of the Eighth Division. The village of Villa Grande menaced their position. Whereupon 19th Brigade moved to the assault, led by 1/5th Essex. Home County men and paratroopers fought from cellar to loft, from one rubble pile to the next. Sometimes they held the same house, breaking through walls and floors to come to grips. Christmas Day saw the fighting rise to climactic bitterness. On the night of December 27th, 5th Royal West Kent Regiment and 1/5th Mahrattas put an end to the struggle by clearing high ground to the north-west of Villa Grande. Next morning only dead Germans and shaken prisoners remained.

Save for some tidying up the battlefield, the first major engagement of the Eighth Indian Division had ended. In the fierce hurly-burly it had borne itself manfully, and had earned high praise from the tough soldiers who fought beside it. But its ordeal was not over with the end of the battle. It continued to man the line in the Adriatic sector throughout three months of abominable winter weather, under continuous stress and strain, and with units much under strength. Finally Spring crept up from the south, and brought warmth to men's bones. It was a time to rest, but there was destined to be no rest. A great battle was in progress sixty miles away, across the Central Apennines. The fighting centred around the massive buttress of Cassino, which commanded one of the two main roads to Rome, and the line of advance into Central Italy. Here the Germans clung fiercely to the strongholds of the Gustav Line. In mid-April the call came for the Eighth Indian Division. Before the end of the month it was concentrated along the River Gari, behind a section of that stream which is better known as the Rapido. Here they met old friends from the Adriatic sector, in the men of the first Canadian Armoured Brigade, which was to serve with them. The task assigned to the Division was to force the Rapido, and to fight to the north-east until the defences of Monte Cassino had been turned. At 2300 hours on May 11th, 600 guns crashed a great weight of shell upon the enemy's position in the

MAHRATTAS attack up a steep hillside.

PUNJABIS use water-course for cover in attack on tough objective.

triangle of valley between the Liri
and the Rapido rivers. Thus opened
the general offensive of 1944, the
greatest battle yet to be fought in
Europe or in Africa. Forty-five
minutes later, the infantry began to
cross the river in assault boats. In a
curtain of smoke and fog, with each
man clinging to the bayonet scabbard

of the man ahead, files of infantry groped forward. The
enemy reacted vehemently. Morning broke on a death
grapple upon the approaches to the main German positions.
Along the river, working furiously, Indian sappers drove out
bridges. One was thrown across under intense artillery and
small arms fire; another was borne on the back of a
Canadian tank, pushed by another tank; thus Canadian and
Indian sappers combined to invent a new type of crossing.
Before nine o'clock, the first Canadian armour was over the
Rapido, and just in time, for panzers had come thrusting up
to deal with our infantry. The Canadians destroyed or held
off the German tanks while the 1st Royal Fusiliers, the 1/12th
Frontier Force Regt., the 3/8th Punjabis and the 1st Argyll
and Sutherland Highlanders, (who had replaced the 1/5th
Essex in 19th Brigade) made good the bridgehead. It was
during this consolidation that Sepoy Kamal Ram of 3/8th
Punjabis volunteered to mop up enemy machine gun nests.
With superb gallantry and judgement he not only slew and
captured the garrison of post after post, but lived to become
the recipient of the Division's first Victoria Cross.

From the bridgehead the 1/5th Gurkhas swept through to
storm San Angelo, a heavily fortified stronghold which was

THE EIGHTH INDIAN DIVISION on the river SENIO, showin
their work. Sepoy ALI HAIDER, 6/13th Royal Frontier Force R
V.C.s it

he burning banks after the 'Crocodiles' and 'Wasps' had done
s, and Sepoy NAMDEO JADHAO, 1st MAHRATTAS, won their
his area.

the key to the river defences. Then 21st Brigade took up the running, and 5th Royal West Kent Regt., 1/5th Mahrattas, and 3/15th Punjabis burst into the main German positions. When Pignataro fell to a Pathan charge at twilight, the breach was complete. General Russell sent a message of congratulation to his tired men, bidding them " rest and lubricate." But rest was far away. The men who had punched the hole were called upon to exploit and to pursue. On an axis east of the main road to Rome, the brigades of the Division began to leapfrog on a drive into the north. For five weeks, for 220 miles the pursuit into the heart of Central Italy was continued by Brigades and 6th D.C.O. Lancers whose speed and dash kept up the momentum of the advance, capturing many bridges intact before the Germans could destroy them. At times only rearguards gave trouble ; at a few points, such as at Veroli and at Guarcino, a set-piece attack was necessary to dislodge the stubborn enemy. This long pursuit tried all ranks of the Division to the utmost, but none more than the R.I.A.S.C. and other maintenance services, whose magnificent efforts enabled the Eighth Division, although starting late in the chase, to finish the pursuit furthest north of all Allied divisions. At the end of June, not far from Perugia, the 17th Brigade stormed Ripa Ridge, in the face of stiff resistance. The enemy now stood at bay. After eight and a half months campaigning, the Eighth Division came out to rest.

On July 26th, at Siena, His Majesty the King pinned on Sepoy Kamal Ram the Empire's supreme award for valour.

The Divisional rest was only a breather before the next round. By July 22nd the Eighth Division had moved 85 miles to the north-west of where it had left the running, still accompanied by their comrades of the Canadian Armoured

HIS MAJESTY the KING inspects Guard of Honour of 3/8th PUNJABIS during his tour of the Italian front.

Brigade. The confidence reposed by the sepoys in Canadian tanks, and by Canadian tankmen in Indian infantry, was heart-moving. When given other armour the Mahrattas enquired with feeling, "Where are our own tanks?" When asked to indicate a regiment for postwar affiliation, the V.C.O.'s of the 3/15th Punjabis unanimously chose the 14th Calgary Armoured Regiment. Nor was this trust and affection unreciprocated. A young Canadian tank officer told a Canadian Press representative: "When they tell us we're going to be fighting with the Indians, we're happy as hell. We hope they feel the same way about us."

Other time-tried Dominion comrades, the New Zealanders, came up on the flank of the Eighth Division as it began to press towards the loop of the Arno River, which lay like a great moat against the city of Florence. On August 12th the 5th Royal West Kent Regiment crossed into the city by Ponte Vecchio, and occupied the area surrounding the Cathedral and the Medici Palace, in the heart of the city. The 21st Brigade assumed command of all troops in Florence, including the Italian partisans. Among services rendered during this occupation was the recovery and safe custody of some of the world's greatest art treasures, including the Botticelli masterpiece " Primavera ".

The Division's next objective was already in sight. East of Florence the Sieve joins the Arno; it sweeps down to the confluence in a great bend along the foothills of the Apennines. Within this bend the Germans held a series of high spurs which constituted the outworks of the Gothic Line, a defence zone designed to bar entry into the narrow valleys by which the roads climb to the crests of the mountains. These formidable fortifications protected the

JAIPUR infantry move up to forward positions.

lateral communications of the enemy and allowed him to transfer troops from one Italian front to another. Should this line be pierced, the Germans would be compelled to retreat through circuitous mountain passes on to the open plains of Northern Italy.

When the Eighth Division concentrated for the assault, it needed above all else room to manœuvre. The Arno crossing was unopposed; the enemy energetically shelled smoke screens laid down to attract attention while the bulk of the Division crossed elsewhere. The 17th Brigade moved forward to probe the outworks of the Gothic Line. The 19th Brigade came up on the left, and found bitter fighting before it could carry its objectives. On September 10th, the assault on the main Gothic positions began. The 21st Brigade carried Monte Cisterna and Monte Veruca, while the 6th D.C.O. Lancers worked up to Gattaia. On September 15th, 17th Brigade surged over Monte Stelletto, pushing on to Femina Morta, in the rear of the main enemy positions. The Gothic Line had cracked.

But although this formidable defence system had fallen more easily than had been expected (perhaps because the enemy considered the terrain too difficult for an attack in strength to be mounted), the great wall of the Apennines still confronted the Indians. Supporting divisions, on either flank, monopolized the only recognizable roads. However, at Marradi, some miles ahead, a main road through the mountains might be seized. Once again, it was a matter of clearing summits to gain room to bring sufficient forces into the line of battle. The 19th Brigade pushed forward, but bad weather delayed operations until October 7th, when 1st Argyll and Sutherland Highlanders captured Monte

MACHINE-GUNNERS wear white camouflage in the snow.

Cavallara. Thus the battle for the Apennine passages began.

For more than two months, in foul and wintry weather, on a mountainous glacis where the available roads were seldom more than jeep tracks, the Eighth Division with its comrades, the British First and Seventy-Eighth Infantry Divisions  and the Sixth Armoured Division, battled grimly upwards and over the crests of the watersheds which barred the way to the plains of Northern Italy. At no time were the Divisional administration services more severely tested, nor showed to better advantage, than in the Herculean task of keeping some thousands of men fed, munitioned and in fighting trim on the bleak rain-swept ridges of the Apennines. The combatant troops needed unfailing and unflinching support in order to make headway. Beyond Monte Cavallara the Casalino Ridge was difficult to take, and even more difficult to hold. Argylls, Jaipur (these splendid State troops in action for the first time), Gurkhas and Punjabis in turn swarmed up this feature, and established themselves, only to be pushed back by venomous counterattacks. So another plan was tried. On the night of October 17th, 3/15th Punjabis and 1/5th Mahrattas infiltrated through the left flank of the divisional position, and in a brilliantly executed attack stormed the heights leading to Pianoereno. They then brought fire to bear on the reverse slopes of Romano Ridge, which barred a frontal advance. This gave elbow room and the Eighth Division began to debouch on the reverse slopes into the eastern foothills of the Apennines.

MAHRATTAS dig in on a 60-ft. flood bank during the historic SENIO river crossing. The enemy is only a few yards away.

Victorious on their own divisional front, the Indians were now in position to assist their neighbours. In order to aid the Polish Corps, on the right, the 1/5th Gurkhas on November 13th stormed Monte Bartolo. Here Rifleman Thaman Gurung, a lone figure on a bullet-swept hilltop, fought to the death to save his platoon and to win a second Victoria Cross for the Eighth Division. On December 1st, the situation of the First British Division, holding Monte Grande, a key position to the north-west, five miles from the Faenza highway and ten miles from the outskirts of Bologna, gave rise to anxiety. 19th Brigade piled into vehicles to begin a two days detour on icy roads so steep that it was often necessary to winch the lorries uphill. The Indians arrived and occupied Monte Grande in time to meet a full-scale German assault. Paratroopers attacked in strength, and bitter fighting ensued in which positions changed hands again and again. In the end wireless intercepts revealed that the enemy had taken such a beating that he could not continue the attack. This Monte Grande fighting was as stubborn and desperate as any of the campaign.

During the three weeks of 19th Brigade's absence, the New Zealanders entered Faenza, and the opposition on the Eighth Divisional front weakened. On December 22nd a dramatic call came. Once again the High Command had anticipated trouble,—this time on the Fifth Army front, where the American 92nd Division held a sector fifteen miles in front of Lucca, a provincial town which covered the main American supply base at Leghorn. 19th and 21st Brigades suddenly found themselves in lorries, skidding their way down the slippery Apennine switchbacks, on a ride one hundred miles to the west. Before they reached Lucca the

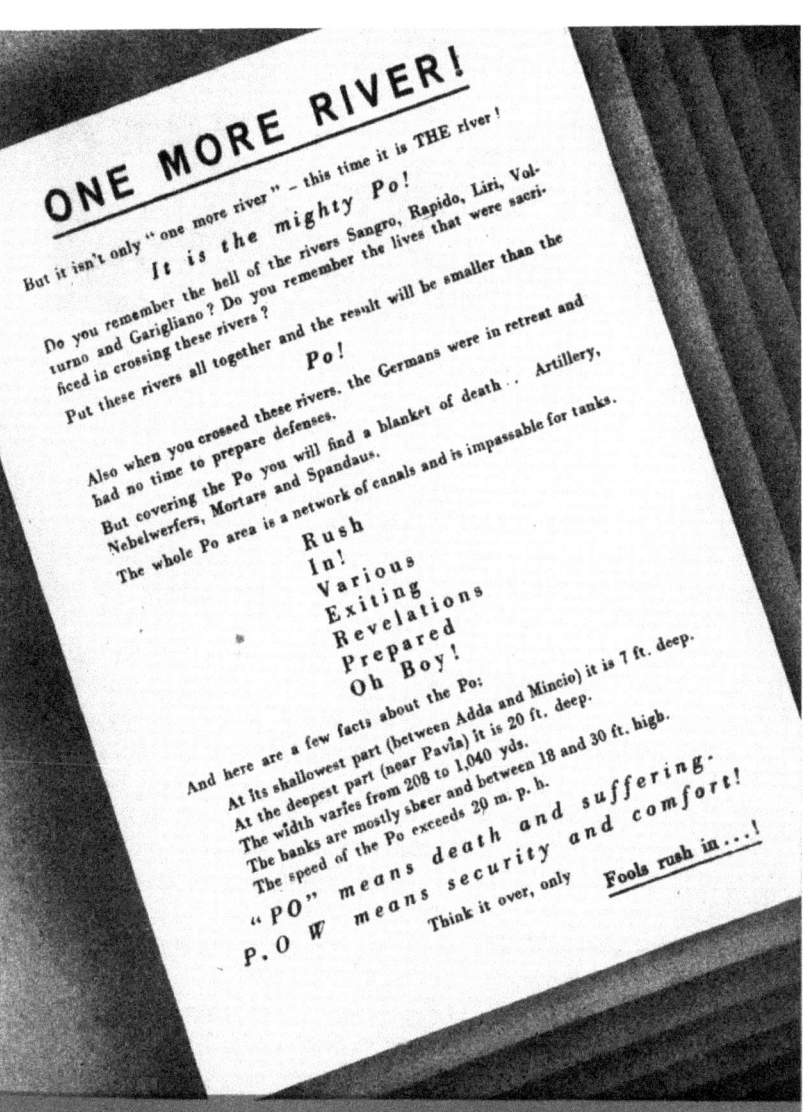

ONE MORE RIVER!

But it isn't only "one more river" – this time it is THE river!

It is the mighty Po!

Do you remember the hell of the rivers Sangro, Rapido, Liri, Volturno and Garigliano? Do you remember the lives that were sacrificed in crossing these rivers?

Put these rivers all together and the result will be smaller than the

Po!

Also when you crossed these rivers, the Germans were in retreat and had no time to prepare defenses.

But covering the Po you will find a blanket of death .. Artillery, Nebelwerfers, Mortars and Spandaus.

The whole Po area is a network of canals and is impassable for tanks.

Rush
In!
Various
Exiting
Revelations
Prepared
Oh Boy!

And here are a few facts about the Po:

At its shallowest part (between Adda and Mincio) it is 7 ft. deep.
At the deepest part (near Pavia) it is 20 ft. deep.
The width varies from 208 to 1.040 yds.
The banks are mostly sheer and between 18 and 30 ft. high.
The speed of the Po exceeds 20 m. p. h.

"PO" means *death and suffering.*
P.O.W means *security and comfort!*

Think it over, only **Fools rush in...!**

WASTE PAPER. This lying leaflet was dropped among Indian troops during the advance to the river PO. It was received with derision.

Germans struck, and the American defences were pierced. General Russell arrived in a fluid sector. Taking personal charge of the battlefield, he cleared away the debris and planted his brigades in the path of the German drive. When the enemy came up against solid bodies, he abandoned the offensive abruptly. By New Year the situation was stabilized, and the Americans once more took over. The Division moved into Pisa for an over-due and well-earned rest, with the Argyll and Sutherland Highlanders leading, in order that they might arrive in time to celebrate their "sacred" occasion of Hogmanay.

The hour of decision now began to loom. For six hundred miles, mountain by mountain, river by river, the Eighth Indian Division, with its comrades of the Eighth Army, had broken every line of defence, had thrust the enemy from every stronghold. Now the mountains were behind, and only a few rivers remained. A vast constricting circle closed around Germany. Once Hitler had struck at the end of each winter. Now spring was handmaiden to the Allies.

In the middle of February the Eighth Division moved back to the Adriatic Coast and relieved Canadians facing the River Senio, twelve miles to the west of the classical city of Ravenna. The Senio was a new sort of river, even to the

Eighth Division. It flowed between floodbanks raised for perhaps thirty feet above the level of the plain. This permitted a system of defence whereby the enemy fortified both banks, and both slopes of both banks, thus making four obstacles out of every river. New defences bred new methods of attack. On the evening of April 9th, when the great assault began with the Eighth Indian Division,

ANSWER to the GERMAN LEAFLET. This 620-ft. bridge was built in 15¾ hours.

the New Zealanders and the Polish Corps as the spearhead of the Eighth Army, 19th and 21st Brigades advanced with forty flamethrowers in close support. These Wasps and Crocodiles curtained the floodbanks in mantles of fire, scorching the enemy in his tunnels and redoubts. The leading battalions, the 1st Argylls, 6/13th Royal Frontier Force Rifles, 1/5th Mahrattas and 3/15th Punjabis, surged across the minefields, clambered over the near bank, swam or waded the river, and threw themselves upon the enemy. The Mahrattas and Frontier Force Rifles in particular encountered fanatical resistance, but two young sepoys, Namdeo Jadhao of the Mahrattas and Ali Haidar of the Frontier Force Rifles, rose to the occasion with superb gallantry.

ENGINEERS of the division helped to construct this 1,370-ft. bridge.

over the river PO. It was the longest floating military bridge in Europe.

Disdainful of death, they charged into a hail of spandau fire, destroyed post after post, and single-handed opened the way for their comrades to sweep the enemy from the floodbanks. Both lived to wear the Victoria Cross.

Close behind the Infantry the sappers rushed up to cut ramps and to assemble bridgework. The Mahratta Anti-Tank Regiment built their bridges of ingenious pattern—cableway ropewalks over which their guns and jeeps were slung rapidly. By dawn the British 21st Tank Brigade was crossing the Senio on three bridges (one of them " Ark " bridge two tanks deep), and were closing up to help the infantry destroy the last desperate groups who sold their lives to delay the breakthrough. That evening the 3/8th Punjabis smashed the faltering defences, and reached the banks of the Santerno. The Jaipurs, the 5th Royal West Kent Regiment and the 6/13th Royal Frontier Force Rifles, widened the gap through which the 17th Brigade entered the battle. The Jaipurs liberated Lugo, with its hideous modernistic statue of Mussolini, the mayor meeting them with a white flag in one hand, a bottle of wine in the other.

On the evening of April 11th, a fearful concentration of guns and bombers rained destruction upon the Santerno positions. Flamethrowers once more seared the weapon pits and hideouts along the floodbanks. The 1/5th Gurkhas and 1/12th Frontier Force Regiment swept across the river, followed by 1st Royal Fusiliers. The crust of resistance crumbled. Once again the tanks came plunging over at

Indian machine-gunner guards NAZI PRISONERS taken during the final assault in Northern Italy.

dawn, to punch through into the open. The spearhead had gouged a gaping wound. The British 78th Infantry and Sixth Armoured Divisions swept through in the wake of the tanks, to join the 56th Division and the New Zealanders in smashing the enemy into the ground at the battle of the Argenta gap.

The Eighth Indian Division, its mission fulfilled, was in no mood to vacate the van of the battle. In the last stages of the Argenta fighting all three Indian brigades thrust through on to Route Sixteen, and raced up to envelope Ferrara, ancient city of swordsmen, with its mediaeval moated fortress in the centre of the town. Beyond Ferrara coiled the Po, mightiest waterway in Italy, but to the Indians only one more river to cross. The pace was accelerating; before a bridge could be built, two thirds of the Division had crossed, ferried on the D.D. Tanks and "Fantails" of Ninth Armoured Brigade. Ten miles beyond the Po, the swiftly flowing Adige supplied the last river line before the Piave in the far north. Still in the van, the Indian sappers built their last bridge, but again too late to serve their own infantry, for the 1/5th Gurkhas and 1/12th Frontier Force Regiment had already crossed, clinging to the swimming tanks. Now came the final mad hours, when infantry and armour raced up the roads, heading for Padua and the exciting prize of Venice. Others were destined to swoop upon these cities; Padua, where milling crowds, frantic with joy, crowded the streets all day long to cheer the troops as they swept through into the north; Venice, calm and queenly to friend and foe alike, and given only to handkerchiefs discreetly waved from windows. Yet the Eighth Division was not unrepresented at the end of a campaign in which it had done everything asked of it, and had often given more for good measure. While German emissaries were presenting themselves at Allied Headquarters to accept a victor's terms, the 6th D.C.O. Lancers darted off on a special mission. Far up on the road to Austria, they came upon their old enemies, the First German Paratroop Division. Whereupon one British officer, two Sikhs, and six Jats arranged to accept the surrender of 11,000 men.

There were now no more rivers—in Italy—for the Eighth Indian Division to cross.

BRITISH and INDIAN troops "brew up" in the ALPS at the end of the arduous campaign.

BRAVEST OF THE BRAVE

SEPOY
KAMAL RAM, V.C.
8th Punjab Regiment.
At the age of 19 he was
the war's youngest V.C.

SEPOY
NAMDEO JADHAO, V.C.
1/5th Mahratha Light Infantry
He won the Decoration in
the Senio river crossing.

SEPOY
ALI HAIDER, V.C., 6/13th
Frontier Force Rifles. He
also was a hero of the
Senio River Battle.

Rifleman THAMAN GURUNG, V.C., 1/5th Royal Gurkha Rifles, was decorated posthumously for his gallantry at Monte San Bartolo in November 1944. Standing in full view of the Germans he covered the withdrawal of his comrades until he fell mortally wounded.

Summary of Approved Honours & Awards Made to 8 Ind. Div. up to 5th June 1945

Award.	Total for Regular Units of the Div.	Total for Units Att. to the Div.	Grand Total.
Awards.			
V.C.	4	..	4
D.S.O.	24	1	25
Bar to D.S.O.	2	1	3
I.O.M.	22	..	22
M.C.	145	15	160
Bar to M.C.	4	..	4
D.C.M.	4	..	4
I.D.S.M.	111	4	115
Bar to I.D.S.M.	1	..	1
M.M.	235	27	262
Bar to M.M.	1	..	1
	553	48	601
Honours.			
C.B.	1	..	1
C.B.E.	2	..	2
O.B.E.	7	..	7
M.B.E.	20	..	20
B.E.M.	4	..	4
	34	..	34
	587	48	635

N.B.—98 recommendations for periodic awards remain outstanding at date of publication.

Battle Casualties While

	KILLED			
	Offrs.	V.C.Os.	B.O.Rs.	I.O.Rs. & N.Cs.E.
Total Casualties from D.B.C.R. Summary Book	91	34	583	1,310
Deduct Non-Div. units less Jewish Bde. (not included)*	1	..	9	19
	90	34	574	1,291
Add :— (a) 6 Lancers when u/c 26 Armd. Bde. (6 Armd. Div.)..	..	..	..	4
(b) 19 Bde. when u/c 1 (Br.) Inf. Div.	..	..	2	13
(c) 1 R.F. when u/c 78 (Br.) Ind. Div.	..	..	3	..
(d) 17 Bde. Gp. when u/c 13 Corps ..	..	..	..	1
	90	34	579	1,309
* Casualties of Jewish Bde. u/c 3-25 March 1945 (Inclusive).	..	..	5	..

In C.M.F. 1943-1945

	WOUNDED				MISSING		
Offrs.	V.C.Os.	B.O.Rs.	I.O.Rs. & N.Cs.E.	Offrs.	V.C.Os.	B.O.Rs.	I.O.Rs. & N.Cs.E.
252	151	2,061	5,641	20	5	394	305
3	..	15	70	..	..	1	..
249	151	2,046	5,571	20	5	393	305
..	1	..	11	..	..	..	..
..	2	9	121	1	..	24	..
..	..	2		..			
..	1	..	25		..	..	1
249	155	2,057	5,728	21	5	417	306
4	..	60	..	..	..	..	..

INDIAN DIVISIONS WON A FINE REPUTATION IN WORLD WAR TWO

Field Marshal Auchinleck, Commander-in-Chief of the British Indian Army from 1942, asserted that the British *"couldn't have come through both wars (World War I and II) if they hadn't had the British Indian Army"*. British Prime Minister Winston Churchill also paid tribute to *"the unsurpassed bravery of Indian soldiers and officers"*.

Between 1945 and 1947, the Director of Public Relations, War Department, Government of India, published a series of short publications covering the individual histories of the WWII Indian Divisions. They followed a consistent format, having between 44 and 48 pages within illustrated soft card covers. They have an average of 50 monochrome photographic illustrations, and each has a full colour centrespread depicting a scene from the Division's wartime operations (drawn by official war artists). They were printed at various presses in Bombay and New Delhi, and each contains at least one map.

As condensed histories they are useful – particularly those which relate to Divisions for which no other record was ever produced.

The British Indian Army during World War II began the war, in 1939, numbering just under 200,000 men. By the end of the war, it had become the largest volunteer army in history, rising to over 2.5 million men in August 1945. Serving in divisions of infantry, armour and a fledgling airborne force, they fought on three continents: in Africa, Europe and Asia.

This Army fought in Ethiopia against the Italian Army, in Egypt, Libya, Tunisia and Algeria against both the Italian and German Army and, after the Italian surrender, against the German Army in Italy. However, the bulk of the British Indian Army was committed to fighting the Japanese Army, first during the British defeats in Malaya and the retreat from Burma to the Indian border; later, after resting and refitting for the victorious advance back into Burma, as part of the largest British Empire army ever formed. These campaigns cost the lives of over 87,000 Indian service- men, while another 34,354 were wounded, and 67,340 became prisoners of war. Their valour was recognised with the award of some 4,000 decorations, and 18 members of the British Indian Army were awarded the Victoria Cross or the George Cross.

RED EAGLES
The Story of the 4th Indian Division
9781474537520

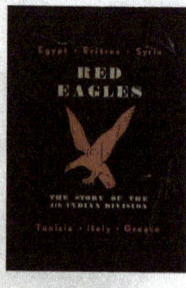

During the Second World War, the 4th Indian Division was in the vanguard of nine campaigns in the Mediterranean theatre, Egypt, Eritrea, Syria, Tunisia, Italy and Greece. The 4th Division captured 150,000 prisoners and suffered 25,000 casualties, more than the strength of a whole division. It won over 1,000 honours and awards, which included four Victoria Crosses and three George Crosses. Field Marshal Lord Wavell wrote: "The fame of this Division will surely go down as one of the greatest fighting formations in military history."

THE FIGHTING FIFTH
History of the 5th Indian Division
9781474537513

As described in much greater detail in Anthony Brett James's book 'The Ball of Fire', the division saw active service in East Africa, North Africa and Burma.

GOLDEN ARROW
The Story of the 7th Indian Division
9781474537506

The role of this division is also duplicated by a much larger work: the book by Brig. M. R. Roberts. However, this booklet gives a good account of Kohima and Imphal and the crossing of the Irrawaddy. In 1945, the division was flown into Siam, so becoming the first Allied formation to re-enter South East Asia.

ONE MORE RIVER
The Story of the 8th Indian Division
Biferno, Trigno, Sangro, Moro, Rapido, Arno, Senio, Santerno, Po, Adige

9781474537490

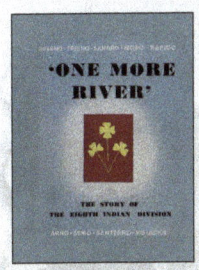

The 8th Indian Division started its overseas service in the Middle East in the garrisoning of Iraq and then the invasion of Persia to secure the oil fields of the area for the Allies, before moving to Italy in 1943. Landing at Taranto, it pushed up the length of the peninsula in a series of major battles: breaking the Sangro Line, forcing the Rapido and turning the defences at Cassino, breaking the stubborn German resistance at Monte Grande and, finally, forcing the Po River. It won four VCs, 26 DSOs and 149 MCs along the way. During the war the 8th Indian Division sustained casualties totalling 2,012 dead, 8,189 wounded and 749 missing.

BLACK CAT DIVISION
17th Indian Division

9781474537483

This formation was committed to Burma from the early days when the British were in full flight from the invading Japanese. It remained in Burma right through to the end, when the starving remnants of the Japanese Army were making their own desperate retreat.

TIGER HEAD
The Story of the 26th Indian Division
Arakan, Ragoon

9781474537452

This is a history of the division said later by the Japanese to have been the opponent which they most feared. The 26th held the Allied monsoon line in the Arakan during two such seasons, repulsing every attack launched against it. Later it made a series of leap-frog landings down the coast to clinch the issue in the Arakan. It was the first division to enter Ragoon, invading the city from the sea.

A HAPPY FAMILY
The Story of the Twentieth Indian Division, April 1942-August 1945

9781474537476

One of the few Indian divisions in the 14th Army trained specifically for the war in Burma. Raised in Bangalore in 1942, it commenced active operations in late 1943 and served from Imphal through to the end. It established the 14th Army's first brigade-head across the Chindwin and its second such brigade-head across the Irrawaddy. Its final task was to round up the Japanese in French Indochina.

THE TWENTY THIRD INDIAN DIVISION
"The Fighting Cock Division"
Burma, Malaya, Java

9781474537469

The Fighting Cock Division is well recorded in the book by Doulton. This book gives coverage of the heavy fighting at the Kohima Battle, the capture of Tamu, the reoccupation of Malaya in August 1945, and then its strange role on the island of Java – concurrently disarming the Japanese garrison, fighting the insurgent Indonesian nationalists, and caring for 65,000 former internees pending the arrival of a new Dutch administration.

TEHERAN TO TRIESTE
The Story Of The Tenth Indian Division

9781783317028

This History deals with the 10th Indian Div's exploits in Iraq (under Maj Gen "Bill" Slim) its role in the Libyan battles leading up to El Alamein, the following two years of garrison duties in Cyprus and Syria, and finally, its fighting services in the Italian campaign (from Ortona onwards).

THE STORY OF THE 25th INDIAN DIVSION
The Arakan Campaign
9781783317585

Formed in Southern India in August 1942 for defence of that area in case of Japanese invasion, the "Ace of Spades" Division had its baptism of fire in Arakan in February 1944. It served throughout the remainder of that campaign the climax being the battle of Tamandu.

Its victorious fight for the Kangaw roadblock was considered by many to have been the fiercest battle of the entire Burma war, while its liberation of Akyab was the first convincing proof to the rest of the world that the tide had turned against the Japanese.

DAGGER DIVISION
The Story Of The 19th Indian Division
9781783317035

Raised in the late 1941, the 19th was the first "standard" Indian Division. Its troops were the first to breach the Japanese defence line in Burma and to raise the flag at Fort Dufferin. It crossed the Chindwin in November 1944, driving on to Mandalay and Ragoon during seven months of continuous fighting. The 19th's exploits are graphically described also in John Masters' personal memoir, *The Road Past Mandalay*.

www.ingramcontent.com/pod-product-compliance
Lightning Source LLC
Chambersburg PA
CBHW041929090426
42743CB00021B/3480